PLACEMENT TEST

Poems by

Ann Curran

MAIN STREET RAG PUBLISHING COMPANY
CHARLOTTE, NC

Copyright © 2005 Ann Curran

Cover photo of Great Blasket Island, Ireland, by Ann Curran

Acknowledgements

The author notes with appreciation the publications that earlier printed the following poems:

Loyalhanna Review, "Religion Lesson"
Commonweal, "At Calvary Cemetery"
Pittsburgh Post-Gazette, "Biddy Early," "Country of Three and a Third Green Fields"
Three Rivers Poetry Journal, "Even the Stones Speak"

Particular thanks to Jim Daniels for his guidance and encouragement and to Gerald Costanzo, both of Carnegie Mellon University; to Sister Mary Donald and Sister Mary Agnes of the Sisters of Charity of Greensburg, Pa., for their clear delight in the writer's earliest efforts; and to Pat and Harry Dolan for introducing the poet to the land of her forebears.

ISBN: 1-59948-002-6

Produced in the United States of America

Main Street Rag
4416 Shea Lane
Charlotte, NC 28227
www.MainStreetRag.com

*For Ed and Cristi Wintermantel,
Mur and Jimmie Curran,
not to mention Gladys Schmitt*

CONTENTS

Near

Placement Test 9
The Burial 10
Involuntary Visit 11
Minutes of the Philosophy Club 12
My First Death 13
Religion Lesson 15
Religious Fervor 16
The San Francisco Option 17
Touch 18
At Sea Off Maui 19
The Change 20
Eyewitness 21
On the Brink 22
Into the Closet 23
At Calvary Cemetery 24

Far

Marking Time and Place 27
Biddy Early 29
Caution in Killarney 30
Country of Three and a Third Green Fields . 31
Even the Stones Speak 33
Farewell with Flowers 34
Long Distance 35
Where Bushmills and Jameson Mix 36
The Monks' Fishing House 37
Poetic Injustice 38
On the Line 39
Report on Holy Ireland 40

Near

PLACEMENT TEST

She wanted to be a stop sign
at three. Halloween, she became
a nighttime sky, quarter moon
atop her head, shooting stars,
Saturn splashed across her navy
night. Once she painted, pasted,
magic-markered wings too large
for a seven-year-old and told
the neighbors it was hard
to be a butterfly lifting
wings over curbs.

Now I deliver her, at thirteen,
to a high school placement test.
Knots of girls measure her—
summer blonde hair to argyle socks—
alarming in a red ski jacket.
She ignores St. Margaret's Mustangs,
jockey-silks drawn together like bits
of metal round a charged pole.
She joins the herd with two
#2 pencils, brown-bag lunch,
skin-deep courage.

In the rain, I watch her down
the glass-walled corridor.
A quick, embarrassed smile
to a mother, whose eyes warm
in the cool, morning air.
At the desk, she removes
the red jacket with a flutter.
I lose her in the pastel clutter
of people getting pigeonholed.

THE BURIAL

Like budding witches they sit
around a blue, autumn fire

deep in the trees at the bottom
of the yard. Three teens plotting

to bury a memory.
Already the ancients guide

their hands. They sprinkle Dad's wine
on the grave. Drop in the love

letter with castle floor plan
from an otherwise bright boy

with braces and persistence.
The tape of his sad lyric.

The dirt. They melt candle stubs
to seal the tomb. They shriek

like banshees when it's all done
and for the moment believe

that memories die
as easily as leaves.

INVOLUNTARY VISIT

In sleep, I go back to that old kitchen.
My mother bellows up the backstairs
to those her silence can wake no more.
She sits at weary attention with cigarette
and coffee in light, too bright.
Or clatters dishes in the sink that hangs
from the wall. I watch her fertility
finally die there in great sudden splashes
of blood on the worn linoleum
where once I imitated death
with ketchup and a bread knife.

Cold, I back against the stove where chestnuts,
always left too long, explode their pus
on the oven's blackened walls.
Her face tells me my robe
is on fire. Her watch, rewarded.
Once more, she shrieks as though defiled
as Cromwell gallops to the backyard
with the Sunday roast in his jaws.
And the girl in the photograph laughs
as she covers that hole in the wall
where all my dreams and nightmares
still pour through.

MINUTES OF THE PHILOSOPHY CLUB

Because the knives were hidden
Daddy in a drunken snit
armed himself with a meat fork.
He sat like some tribal chief
demanding answers from me
about life, love, God.

I wore a royal blue dress
with a stripe of red across
the chest. When Mother came
he rose and roared. Three red dots
splashed shock across my blue.

MY FIRST DEATH
For "Gentleman Jim" Scanlan

Even in his eighties
he filled doorways
and left tall men
shrinking in his shadow.

They say he knocked out
Jack Johnson with one punch.
At our house he drank
Cambridge tea—hot water
with sugar and cream.

They say he took grandma's rings
for safekeeping
and never gave them back.
She sewed violets around
his greenhorn portrait.

They say he never married
the woman he loved
but kept her picture
in a trunk in the attic
and spent hours there.

He came from Kerry,
everyone knew, but years
later his daughter said,
no, she felt sure
it was East Liberty.

He seemed a heaving mound
when he lay dying
in the corner of a ward.
We kept our coats on
waiting for him to go.

When the noises came,
no nurse rushed in
to pound or shock life
back into that ancient chest.
We went away without tears.

RELIGION LESSON

Down the side aisle of my childhood
I walked in endless procession
flowering stone floors with torn blooms

chanting unknown words to a God
hidden behind incense and male
voices. But I breathed in beauty

in the rise of song, the fall of
petals, the Roman arches strong
as the promise of forever.

I believed in beauty first.
God was easy after that.

RELIGIOUS FERVOR

It was the way he folded
his fingers together
the dark spark in his eyes
the steady rhythm
in his little talks
the only voice
that didn't wear
rosary beads.
It sent the 12-year-old girls
off to the rectory
at lunch break
to bring him down
from his private prayers
to murmur his magic
over their medals
bought with milk money.

THE SAN FRANCISCO OPTION

You touch my hair like a child
pats an unfamiliar pet
that's soft, lovely, likely
to bite. You retreat, admire
from the other corner
of the back seat. At the park
we leave the dance, run wildly
up the wooded hill to talk
in a clearing, blind to stars.
You hold me at a distance.
When we kiss, you're a brother.
Later, I meet your lover
and want you no less, I guess.

TOUCH

In that distance
between where you are
and where I am
is darkness
that burns
behind the eyes.
When your lips cross
my body
light explodes
like a stream
down a hillside
taking six paths
across the asphalt
ignoring all boundaries.

AT SEA OFF MAUI

I crawl into this dark berth
rocking with waves
that splash against memory.

I brought my mother
dying in a wheelchair
to these islands.
She exchanged her cigarettes
for oxygen, determined
to see one last time
her only child
not born perfect.

We flew west
into yesterday
and found him,
the sergeant
with the funny lip,
steeled against all softness
but least prepared
to handle any more hurt.

THE CHANGE

As the ovaries wither
a strange fire burns
along the veins.

A man in rubber gloves
predicts the pre-dawn hour
when I'll awake
wet with sweat.
And I awake
wet with sweat.

I walk thirty miles
in anger from a minor offense
I can't quite recall.

I laugh beyond
the edge of control,
throat scalding,
sound breaking
halfway between
a snort and a sob.

EYEWITNESS

Sometimes I try to kill
a floater in my eye
when it blips across
my optic nerve looking
like a fast gnat
flying in my face.
And I understand
how thousands can watch
a pope or president shot
and no two agree
on what happened.

Sometimes the doctor
looks inside my eye
with special lens.
In the mirror of that glass
I see backwards.
Bloody branches
feed that dark core
that carries upside down
pictures to my brain.
Sometimes I adjust them.

ON THE BRINK

We paddled inner tubes
across Rock Bottom,
shivered in the shadows
of the cliff, told tales
of bodies bobbing
up dark nights. Brave
in the blue atop
that hill we slid over
the edge, feet found
the one safe ledge
above the black pool.

In another country
lying on a narrow shelf
above the sea, too high
to hear the white beat
against fallen boulders,
we move in reckless
rhythm while the wind
screams through sunshine.
There is no other time,
no other place,
no end, ever.

Now even in your warmth
I watch a host go singly
to that final cliff,
and I shrink before
the slightest height
as though being careful
could save me.

INTO THE CLOSET

Death comes quietly to our house.
A sob swells in the throat,
never reaches the tongue,
never tears the air.

Arms grasp in unfamiliar embraces.
We grieve in walk-in closets,
nails ripping through
flower-shrouded shelves.

We select coffins sensibly,
put mourners in proper order,
endure their remembrances,
and bury our pain—

only to feel it rise
again and again.

AT CALVARY CEMETERY

The gardener directs:
"Go up here a little piece.
You'll see Jesus
his hand up like this.
Turn left."
If I see Jesus
his hand up like this,
I'll move right
to the middle of the road,
play the odds, suck up
for kingdom come.

My father lies
in two plots
if you believe
the stones. Mother moved
his bones wanting no part
of "those Currans."
When her turn came,
no one erased his name.

I'll lie down
with three cousins,
last of the indentured
Irish slaves who gave
up their mansions
for this modest space.
Almost a century spans
their days and deaths.
"Nothing there by now,"
the cemetery director
says. "One body.
You'll fit easily."
Small comfort.

Far

MARKING TIME AND PLACE

Many ascetic monks of the early Irish church, recognizing that their love for Ireland was so close to physical love, felt a penitential need to exile themselves from their lovely island.
—Brian de Breffney in *The Land of Ireland*

We dream in calendars.
I buy Ireland. Each week
I turn the page to see
where I would rather be.

A purple day in Galway.
Connemara calling
me to its rugged wastes,
its accidental lakes.

A single red boat waits
in the high grass in Sneem
to carry me through reeds
and silence to Kerry

where a ring of ancient
stones stands undisturbed
by farmers hedging bets
against the older gods.

I'm even suckered by
a thatched-roof cottage
dug into a soft hillside
in Donegal, the top

of the Irish world, sky
bending low, cloud-close,
air, sharp as wits milking
cows feet deep in dung.

Men in black suits and rubber
boots tear turf from the earth
to burn eyes and warm hearts.
Sun in Clare makes beach towns glare.

The Atlantic bends trees
into a black blur.
The sea smacks Dun Laoghaire
with white anger. The taste

of salt rides every breeze.
In this white-washed world,
green beneath shattered churches,
wet beyond belief

I do not see small lives,
small places, grey towns,
grey faces. I see
where I began.

BIDDY EARLY

They called her the witch of Clare,
a red-headed herbalist

who cured coughs and falling hair,
brewing tea from turnips, cat

mint, moss, thyme. The devil's snare
snarled the nervous, local priest.

So when we relieved ourselves
behind her thatched-roof cottage

and laughed at spells and green elves,
she struck with a vengeance rare.

CAUTION IN KILLARNEY

I always want to pull
you from the path
at Muckross Abbey

beside Killarney's lakes,
drag you into the bushes,
play Ryan's daughter,

watch the treetops throb,
the spider web swell
in and out with the wind

as we listen to lust
in the flowered brush.
But you fear the freckled folk

pushing through the woods
looking for rare flora,
not bare fauna.

We return to the path
and burn all the way back
to cold sheets, high ceilings.

COUNTRY OF THREE AND A THIRD GREEN FIELDS

Country of teen-age pickets
snickering at their own strike.
Country of old men in black suits
on black bikes pedaling through the green.
Country of myths as farfetched
as Columbus in Galway,
Lynch lynching his own son
for honor's sake. Country of poets
revered and exiled; of legends
inhaled with turf smoke; of cows, donkeys,
sheep cluttering narrow roads.
Country of divided churches.
Christ crucified in fresh farm faces.
Country of customs that ape the enemy.

Country of seas that never cease
to play with minds, luring them
toward the orange edge of promise.
Country of stacked stones making plots
too small to lie down and die in.
Country of castles haunted
with yesterday's hatreds.
Country of green hills, valleys
and no green people. Country of harps
slung over slim shoulders marching
down backstreet Dublin. Country of song
and singing violins, swollen
with rain and torment.
Country of sailors who cannot swim,
of fishermen in love with the deep.
Country of round towers piercing
damp skies, of still lakes calling

sentimental tourists home,
of mists adrift on mountain roads.
Country of Geralds, Jeremiahs,
Tim, Tom, Danny, Margaret, Bridget,
Nora, Annie. Country of bogs, blarney,
redheads, thatched roofs, dirt, damp,
talk and eternal mockery.
Country of shamrocks torn from garden walls
and mailed abroad. Country of clothes
drying in the rain, of meat cooled
in the well, of barefoot children
running off to Australia.

Country of cow dung and lace curtains,
lace curtains and cow dung.
Country of creameries and cousins
in every land. Country of pale
priests and sour housekeepers.
Country of minds that saw no dark ages.
Country of lust stamped out on wooden floors
by nervous peasant boys. Country
of foreign tongues, rosary beads,
vigil lights. Country of poached salmon,
too many potatoes, apple tarts,
home-grown gypsies, warm dark beer.

Country of Munster, Leinster,
Connaught and not enough,
Lord God, not enough, of Ulster.

EVEN THE STONES SPEAK

In this cobble
collected on an Irish shore,
I feel the comforting chill
of summer in a milder land,
the throb of a heart
longing to go home.
I watch the Atlantic lift,
curl and toss
this broken token
on a troubled island.
I carry this stone
like some confused Goliath
struck once and forever
by the indestructible dream
of some perfect place.

FAREWELL WITH FLOWERS
For Joseph O'Curraidhin of Spiddal, Ireland

He stood by the turf fire
the frost of death

already touching his frame—
rigid with pain.

Eyes staring beyond
the moment. Smile

out of tune with the talk.
A baby buggy crowding

his corner of the cottage.
He crawled from bed to see

the Yanks one more time
and sent them off

with two daffodils
snatched from his last garden.

LONG DISTANCE

I talk to you in another time.
Your words cross days, a generation,
an ocean. Your red-headed toddlers
wear the British uniform. I pray
my Catholic relatives will not
bloody your lives. Unless they have to.
I pray we may talk across the dark
till both of us have vanished.
I pray you forget to blame me.
I can handle no further distance.

WHERE BUSHMILLS AND JAMESON MIX
For Sarah Buckley

I never understood drinking
till that cold Irish summer
when we flopped on great soft
sofas before Buckleys' turf fire
sipping whiskey while the world
narrowed to our space
flickering a peasant
pleasantness on every face.

THE MONKS' FISHING HOUSE

Eight hundred years of water
have passed beneath the stone house
on the River Cong where monks
once answered the bell that rang
when confused and hurried trout
were caught in the clerics' trap.

The fish would circle, circle
in the watery cell below
the floor till a monk would come
to free it for supper
and forever. Toward the end
of the abbey's days, High-King

Roddy O'Connor himself
came to visit. He didn't catch
any fish. In fact he stayed
fifteen years and died on that
isthmus between Lough Corrib
and Lough Mask. Blessed Ireland
then buried its last high king.

POETIC INJUSTICE

Padraic O Conaire sits
at the top of Eyre Square
hat pushed back, eyes lowered
to his last poem.
One bronze foot stands on the other.
A seagull shits down his back.
Just behind him there
all the youth of Europe
toss Ireland's first, fast-food
wrappers across the green.

ON THE LINE

Cavanaugh came strutting down
from Donegal, black hair
slicked back, blue eyes
pretending innocence,
second-hand tweed suit
to awe the country folk.

Hunkered down in barnyards,
peeping over clergy specs,
he guessed the Kerry farmers
ought to know the phone company
was after rerouting lines.
If they acted now, today,

those poles were theirs
for fences, cow stalls, firewood.
Timber like that was seldom seen
in treeless Ireland.
Five pounds apiece.
They tripped through dung

to deliver their savings
from biscuit tins
and take an official receipt.
Three hundred poles later
two farmers claiming their wood
hacked Kerry into silence.

Cops caught Cavanaugh
singing in the local pub.
He sobbed all the way to jail
about the boat he needed
to make a decent living
for himself and his mother.

REPORT ON HOLY IRELAND
He can take his effing report and stick it up his arse.
　　　　　　　　　　　　The Irish Times, July 1999

On the buses, lads and lassies sport
Levi Strauss, Adidas, Nike clothes.
In a pub chubby four and five-year-olds
raise their baby bottles
sucking artificial nipples.
In the Gaeltacht, language
students learn Irish
from people who speak
English all day long.
In Spiddal, the government
has ceased dumping
shit in Galway Bay
and built a poo-processing plant.
Only the stink shall sink them now.
In the churches, Irish baffles
even more than Latin.
The faithful bow
their heads in private prayer.
Others damn the clergy
for assaulting children,
for building mansions
to live and pray in.
The poet, a secular priest,
announces his penchant for boys.